# Our new house

### Photography by Bill Thomas

Dear Tim,

We are in our new house now.

Dear Tim,
We are in our new house now.

We have boxes
all over the place.

Dear Tim,
We are in our new house now.
We have boxes all over the place.

I like going up and down
the stairs in our new house.

Dear Tim,

We are in our new house now.
We have boxes
all over the place.
I like going up and down
the stairs in our new house.

My bedroom is at the top of the stairs.

Dear Tim,

We are in our new house now.
We have boxes
all over the place.
I like going up and down
the stairs in our new house.
My bedroom is at the top
of the stairs.

# My toys are in my bedroom.

Dear Tim,

We are in our new house now.
We have boxes
all over the place.
I like going up and down
the stairs in our new house.
My bedroom is at the top
of the stairs.
My toys are in my bedroom.

I can see my new school from my window.

Dear Tim,

We are in our new house now.
We have boxes all over the place.
I like going up and down the stairs in our new house.
My bedroom is at the top of the stairs.
My toys are in my bedroom.
I can see my new school from my window.

I can walk to my new school.

Dear Tim,

We are in our new house now.
We have boxes
all over the place.
I like going up and down
the stairs in our new house.
My bedroom is at the top
of the stairs.
My toys are in my bedroom.
I can see my new school
from my window.
I can walk to my new school.

Dear Tim,
We are in our new house now.
We have boxes all over the place.
I like going up and down the stairs in our new house.
My bedroom is at the top of the stairs.
My toys are in my bedroom.
I can see my new school from my window.
I can walk to my new school.
You can come and stay with me.
From Billy